Language for a "Catholic" Church
A Program of Study

— Revised and Updated —

Thomas H. Groome

Sheed & Ward

Sheed & Ward™ is a service of National Catholic
Reporter Publishing Company, Inc.

Library of Congress Catalog Card Number: 91:60173

ISBN: 1-55612-408-2

Published by: Sheed & Ward
                115 E. Armour Blvd.
                P.O. Box 419492
                Kansas City, MO 64141-6492

To order, call: (800) 333-7373

Contents

Preface to a Program

What is "inclusive language?" Why should we consider using it? How does one go about doing so? These are the questions this handbook addresses.

For some who have long ago responded to this issue and either rejected the whole idea as a passing fad, even a threat of heresy, or embraced the notion and adjusted their language pattern accordingly, these may sound like "tired" questions. But to experience Sunday liturgy in a sampling of churches will readily indicate that they are still "timely," even urgent. Too many parishes seem not to have addressed the issue at all (would 75% be an exaggeration?), and Catholic congregations appear to sin more boldly with exclusive language than do mainline Protestant ones. There is great need in many parishes for educational programs that help people to address the very language they use as persons and as communities of faith. Undoubtedly we have here a controversial issue and this small volume takes a strong stand on the side of embracing "inclusive" language for ourselves and "expansive" language for God. Yet my hope is that its conversational style and program format can be a resource to enable people to address their language "together in love."

This issue presents faith communities and their religious educators with an eminently "teachable moment"; an appropriate response can have far-reaching ripple effects on the faith life of a parish. The issue of inclusive language goes to the very heart of our "catholicity" and sacramentality as the Body of Christ. It tests our conversion to being a community that welcomes all and includes everyone, and measures our "catholicity" in the very language we use of ourselves and God in our prayer, worship, and catechesis. Many people experience the issue of inclusive language as a threatening or emotion-laden one; few can approach it dispassionately. All the more reason, then, that it be addressed through a sensitive, respectful and consciousness-raising educational process, one that itself reflects the values of inclusion, dialogue and participation.

In the three chapters that follow, I offer the outline of a program that can enable a parish community or a group within it to address the issue of inclusive language, and to do so as an event of faith education. I have presented an abbreviated version of this program in a two-hour workshop, and what is contained here can be similarly adapted. For a more complete program, however—and since the theme lends the opportunity to raise other faith education issues—I propose three sessions (approximately 2 hours each) corresponding to the three chapters of this handbook.

I write from and to my own Catholic community of faith, but I hope people and communities of various traditions may also find it a resource. Though I have added to the bibliography of this second edition some fine essays by dissenting voices, I make no pretense at all of the stereotypical "balance" of scholarship that "gives both sides" of the argument. I do have great empathy for people who resist the whole notion; our language patterns are so deeply rooted in our very being that this is like the proverbial asking the leopard to change its spots. However, here I take for granted that people interested enough to be reading this handbook are already committed or well disposed to inclusive language. But what if you had opportunity (by invitation or your own initiative) to sponsor a workshop on inclusive language in your parish, school, etc.? How would *you* proceed? It was such an opportunity that originally prompted me to bring together what follows. I offer it as a resource that people can draw upon, especially with a community beginning to address the issue.

Within each chapter, summary statements are highlighted; these could be put on an overhead transparency or on a handout for participants. Religious educators will likely notice that the overall dynamics of the three envisioned sessions reflect the movements of a "shared Christian praxis" approach to faith education.

In brief, the program begins with a "focusing activity"; here this is done by an opening statement establishing the theme of inclusive language as a "generative" one (Freire) for a Christian community, and particularizing the issue around "gender-inclusivity." The focusing act can also be done in many other ways— a story, an example, a short film, etc.; and facilitators will likely need to "re-focus" the theme at the beginning of sessions 2 and 3. The focusing act leads to an invitation to participants to name *present praxis* (i.e. how they and their communities are responding) regarding the theme, and to critically *reflect* on it (movements 1 and 2). A series of reflections and reasons for inclusive language are offered (movement 3, *Story*), and then some suggestions for how to adjust present language patterns accordingly (movement 3, *Vision*). Here I imagine these resources being made accessible in the second part of session 1, throughout 2, and the beginning of 3. Linkage and appropriation questions are suggested throughout to maintain the dynamics of the program over three sessions. (For a two-hour program, the interspersed questions can be used selectively and the Story/Vision movements condensed). The program concludes (session 3B) with dialogue around questions that prompt participants to "make their own" and appropriate what was presented to their lives and context (movement 4), and offers a more explicit opportunity for personal and communal decision-making (movement 5).[1]

Excerpts from what follows have already been published in *PACE* (No. 20, Dec. 1990 and Jan. 1991). I thank its co-editor, Dr. Padraic O'Hare for very helpful editorial suggestions and enthusiastic support for this handbook. I thank Bob Heyer of Sheed & Ward for publishing this small volume in the first place, and now for encouraging a second edition; it reflects his own deep commitment to the "catholicity" of the Church. I thank Peter C. Finn of the International Commission on

English in the Liturgy (ICEL) for a number of very helpful conversations and suggestions. I thank my spouse, Colleen M. Griffith, for reading the manuscript, and much more for being the primary catalyst in my ongoing journey toward inclusion and mutuality.

Thomas H. Groome
Boston College
Feast of All Saints, 1994

– 1 –

Inclusive Language: A Crucial Issue for Becoming "Catholic"?

"God made man in his image and likeness." How often have you heard some such translation of Genesis 1:27? Its intent is to teach the amazing, inspiring, and dignifying truth of our faith that all of us are made by God, in the image and likeness of our Creator. But implicitly it also conveys that God is a person of male gender and that "man" is the paradigm of human being. (Note too that many contemporary scholars of the Hebrew scriptures agree that it is also a poor—some would even say erroneous—translation of the original text). Oh indeed, women can recognize that they are included in its truth, but they must first pause and interpret whether or not this is so, since they are not explicitly named. And in the subconscious, where such metaphoric language is most effective, the implication remains that, really, "man" most reflects the Creator.

Although inclusive language has been a social issue for more than twenty years, it remains a controversial one, or now, it seems, most often an avoided topic throughout Church and society. There are aspects of English that make it a particularly complex and challenging problem to solve (more below); but for all, "our native language is like a second skin, so much a part of us we resist the idea that it is constantly changing. . . ."[1] Having been socialized into an excluding language pattern, adopting an inclusive one requires deliberate attention and self-reflection, conviction about its importance, practical guidelines for how to proceed, and a bit of practice.

Inclusive language has special urgency for pastoral ministers, religious educators, and all who participate in shaping the public discourse of the Church.

We belong to a faith community that values words, and especially the word of God that comes to us through sacred scripture. We believe that God created through the power of God's word; that in the fullness of time God's word was made flesh in Jesus, the Christ. We are, then, a people with deep respect for the power of our "religious" words, the words that nurture and express our faith. But we must realize that precisely because they have the power to create and heal, when misused our "religious" words can hurt and destroy. How important it is, then, for us to be *care*-ful with our words, and especially our "God talk."

Our Christian faith demands commitment to justice, to peace, to fullness of life for all, to "do the truth with love." We are to teach and preach the universality of God's love, and to foster communities of faith that are sacraments of God's reign, in other words, effective and credible signs of the shalom and fullness of life that God desires for the world. All Christians are to be "catholic," and some of us even claim it as title for our community of faith. Perhaps James Joyce (in *Finnegan's Wake*) captured best the meaning of this word as an adjective; he said "Catholic means here comes everybody." But can we realize and model an inclusive community when we use language that potentially excludes or stereotypes, demeans or diminishes, offends or hurts anyone? Professional and academic groups as diverse as the Society of Automotive Engineers and the American Psychological Association have developed guidelines for inclusive language; what a sad reflection it would be if Christians who profess "catholicity" were to be indifferent to the issue. The fact is that *the purposes of our ministry and the commitments of our faith can be defeated or enhanced by the very language we use.* As Christian persons we are called to speak inclusively because our language "has to do with the most basic matters of faith and with the very possibility of Christian community."[2]

What Is Inclusive Language?

Inclusive language reflects that all people are full human beings with equal value and dignity; it avoids excluding, demeaning or stereotyping anyone on any basis; its personal images for God reflect analogously all humanity, without favor to any.[3]

Excluding and discriminatory language can be based on gender, race, physical ability, class, nationality, religion, social status, and so on. For example, we should use language that reflects positive appreciation of the abilities of physically challenged people and at the same time avoid all "pity" terms (e.g., "unfortunate," "afflicted by," "victim of "). It is "inclusive" in the humanizing sense to say that John "uses a wheelchair" instead of ". . . is confined to a wheelchair," or that "Mary walks with crutches" instead of ". . . is crippled." Likewise, people with any social consciousness know to avoid racist language, i.e., statements, stories, epithets, or pejorative references that stereo-type, put down, exclude, trivialize, or imply the dependency or inferiority of other people on the basis of race or ethnicity. A more subtle form of racism needs to be weeded out of the language patterns traditionally used by religious educators. We should not use color as a pejorative or exalting term as in "black" to imply dirty, sinful, or menacing, (remember those "black" marks on our souls before confession?), and "white" as being clean, pure, or sinless, (and "white" souls afterward!). Similar examples can be cited regarding class, age, religion, etc.[4] And rooting out anti-semitism from our language is a particular responsibility of Christians since we have caused so much of it.

The focus of these reflections, however, is on gender-inclusive language, because: 1) numeri-cally, it refers to and has consequences for the most people; 2) ecclesially, it pertains to what is likely *the* major institutional vice of the Church—sexism; 3) unlike other forms of "abu-sive" language, a gender-excluding pattern of discourse is now built into the very structure of English (e.g., it has no inclusive third person singular personal pronoun). But this excluding pattern is not "accidental" to the language, and certainly not "dropped from heaven." Miller and Swift write: "Much of the unconscious bias embedded in modern English stems from cultural attitudes toward women and, to a lesser but significant extent, from cultural expectations damaging to men."[5] The hope is that to challenge and root out such pervasive and entrenched "excluding" language will heighten peoples' consciousness and cause them to act against not only sexism but every form of prejudice and discrimination. Hardesty writes, "On a human level, an effort to use more inclusive language makes us aware not only of our sexism, but also of our racism, elitism, nationalism, classism, ageism, homophobia, and all our other prejudices."[6]

Questions for Conversation

What is *your* attitude toward the issue of gender-inclusive language?

What do you do about it in your own speech patterns?

How does your faith community respond to this issue?

Explain to yourself some of the "causes" (personal, social, cultural, religious, etc.) of your attitudes and practices.

Explain the attitudes and practices of your community.

Teaching Note. These suggested questions and others throughout will likely need to be adapted and selected according to context, participants, etc. It may help if people have writing materials to note their responses. Pose the questions separately, leaving time for reflection. If time is limited, use one of the first three and one of the second two questions. It may also help to have them on a handout or overhead so that participants can review them during their silent reflection. Conversation and sharing of responses can be done after each one or after all are completed. If the number of participants is large, it will be advisable to separate into smaller groups of three or four people, with summary insights then invited from each small group to enhance the whole group consciousness. Similar procedures are fitting to the "questions for conversation" suggested throughout.

Reasons for Gender-Inclusive Language

Historical

The historical evidence is that *gender-exclusive English originated from and was intended to maintain the conviction that men are "superior" to women and are the "natural" norm of humanity.* One often hears a defense of the allegedly generic terms like "man," "mankind," "him," etc., as if they have always referred to both sexes when that is the intent of the speaker, and that this is an "innocent" arrangement, made simply for convenience, clarity, or aesthetics; many people even argue that such "generic" words are essential to the structure of the English language.

There is no historical warrant at all for these claims; in fact, the evidence is to the contrary. Ironically, both "old English" (c. 500 to c. 1000) and "middle English" (c. 1100 to c. 1500) were more gender-inclusive than "modern English." For example, both had the gender specific words *wif* and *wir* (from latin *vir*) for adult woman and man, and did not use "man" to mean humankind but only adult male. Thereafter, there is clear historical evidence that the shift to such androcentric (male-favoring) language was tied to the myth of male superiority and was intended to reinforce male social power.[7]

One Thomas Wilson, an English grammarian, was apparently the first to make the argument, in 1553, that male "superiority" should be reflected in the patterns of the language. He contended that men should always be named ahead of women and with primary status (as in "man and wife") because of males' "natural" supremacy. In 1646, Joshua Poole, another

grammarian, argued similarly that male terminology should have "pride of place" in language
because the male gender is "the worthier" one.
In 1746, John Kirby built on such sentiment
and went beyond it when he composed his very
influential "Eighty-Eight Grammatical Rules."
Among them, Rule 21 proposed that male
terms such as "man," "mankind," etc., be used
as generic because the male gender is "more
comprehensive" than the female and because
its superiority as the norm of humanity should
be reflected in the English language. Since
Kirby's proposal was widely accepted, there
flowed from it a host of other constructs that
favored men and demeaned women (e.g., Mr.
and Mrs. *John* Smith, emerged late 18th century).

The linguistic legitimation of androcentrism
was encoded into law in 1850 when an act of
the English Parliament decreed that, hence-
forth, "he" legally stands for "she" as well.
This grammatical edict helped reinforce a similar language pattern in other English-speaking
countries, and yet throughout the English-
speaking world "he" continued to be interpreted selectively to favor men. For example,
in 1879 a proposal to admit women to the
all-male Massachusetts Medical Society was
rejected on the grounds that "he" in the Soci-

ety's by-laws on membership referred exclusively to males.[8]

Important to note is that the grammarians, parliamentarians and doctors making these decisions were all men, since women were excluded from such professions. Note also that the history of modern English is not without a few subversive memories of inclusion. For example, the *Oxford English Dictionary* of 1654 proposed the term "spokeswoman" when the spokesperson is a woman, and the *O.E.D.* of 1699 recommended that "chairwoman" be used when a woman so functions. There is ample evidence, however, that our allegedly generic but androcentric language was indeed "man-made" and to men's advantage.

The debilitating legacy left by these historical "developments" can be stated as follows: *in present language patterns, "man" is presumed to be the equivalent of humanity, whereas "woman" is never so. Instead, women are designated a subgroup within humankind, and must interpret whether or not they are included in particular statements.* In our present language patterns men are defined by their humanity, whereas women are defined by their sex—"woman" never means humankind. Linguistically, it is a "man's world" in which women have "a place." Men always know that they are included when such terms as men, man or mankind are used, whereas women must translate and interpret whether or not they are referred to. Sometimes it is obvious, sometimes it is not. On one particular Sunday of late, I heard three apparently different uses of the word "men" in church: "God made all men equal"; "God calls men to the priesthood"; "We need a few strong men to help move the pulpit after Mass." When and how did the women present feel included?

Philosophical

Male-centered language encourages people to interpret their "world" to favor males and lends a sense that this is as it should be. For over two thousand years, the Western world accepted without question the ancient (some would say Aristotelian) philosophy of language that saw it simply as a tool of communication, a neutral medium through which people externalize to others their thoughts, feelings, attitudes, etc. It simply lets people know what one is thinking. This understanding of language as an innocent medium for conveying communication is now strongly rejected as partial and naive because *language shapes as well as expresses what and how we think.*

Contemporary philosophy is marked by a "linguistic turn," meaning particular attention to how the language we use shapes the way we interpret life and the very "world" we know and create for ourselves. Since Kant, philosophers have come to agree that so much of what we know is by our own construction, that the perspective we bring to life greatly shapes what we "see" and the meaning we make out of it. Contemporary linguistic philosophy builds on Kant's insight and argues convincingly that most significant to our "knowledge" are the words we use to describe, categorize, and interpret our lives in the world. Our language shapes how and what we know, our whole philosophy of life. Dale Spender writes, "one of the crucial factors in our construction of 'reality' is language."[9] In consequence, we don't ever "grasp things as they really are." Instead, we see them as our language enables us to name and interpret them.

Linguistic philosophy, then, confronts us with the realization that our "world view"—our philosophy of life, is shaped and biased by our language; further, the "taken for grantedness" of our language pattern lends a kind of assurance that "reality" is as we name it. Spender explains: "Language is not neutral. It is not merely a vehicle which carries ideas. It is itself a shaper of ideas. . . . What we *see* in the world around us depends in a large part on the principles we have encoded in our language."[10] Clearly, then, language that "encodes" principles of male superiority and preference encourages both men and women to "see" and interpret their world accordingly, and as if that's how things are and should be.

Social Sciences

Words are social/cultural symbols that both express and shape our "selves" and "world." The insight of linguistic philosophy—that language shapes our knowledge and way of interpreting life—is verified and expanded by the more empirical research of psychologists, sociologists and anthropologists. A common insight of these social sciences is that the social/cultural context in which we live provides us with shared patterns of meaning, attitudes and values. Further, we come into our self-identity (i.e., self-image, world view and value system) by being socialized into our particular cultural context. Socialization is the process of interiorizing and taking in as our own the patterns of meaning, attitudes, and values proposed to us by our society and culture. The social sciences attest, however, that *the* most powerful media of socialization are the symbols of a culture; our social "world" both expresses and perpetuates itself through its symbols. In other words, by coming to use and interiorize the symbols of our culture we take on its attitudes, values, and world-view. The social sciences now recognize that language is our primary symbol system, in other words, the language we use is the most powerful influence in shaping who we are—our very self identity.

As powerful symbols, words express our cultural "world" and sense of identity; likewise, they influence and shape our sense of "self" and "world." Words "work both ways"—we shape them and they shape us. In this light we must remember that "every language reflects the prejudices of the society in which it evolved, and English evolved through most of its history in a male-centered, patriarchal society."[11] In consequence, its sexist and excluding language patterns both express and help to maintain a world that is patriarchal, and encourage people in attitudes, opinions, disvalues, etc., that are discriminatory toward women. Conversely, because there is a two-way dialectic between our words and ourselves—both expressing us and forming us—gender-inclusive language can help to reform patriarchal social structures and misogynist psyches, and to create social worlds and personal identities that are committed to mutuality, partnership and inclusion.

Questions for Conversation

What is your response to the notes above on the history of male-centered language?

Can you share some personal experiences of how the power of words can shape our knowledge and ourselves? What are some social implications of this insight?

What do you imagine would be some of the eventual consequences if our whole Church began using inclusive language?

What would be your own next step toward such a reality?

− 2 −

Biblical and Other Reasons for Gender-Inclusive Language in the Church

---

Questions for Conversation

What are your own thoughts and feelings about the predominantly male-centered language of the Bible?

What do you think are some of the causes of the Bible's gender-exclusive language for both humankind and God?

Do you imagine such language has any real consequences for the lives of the Bible's readers and hearers? Does God intend those consequences?

Reasons for
Gender-Inclusive Language in the Church

Scriptural

Confessing Christians believe they can discern the "word of God" for their lives through the words of sacred scripture, that its origins, collecting, and editing were inspired by God's Holy Spirit. Our scriptures are most foundational in shaping the words we use to express our faith. By way of inclusive language and the Bible, the issue, on first impression, would appear to be a closed case, a "no go" area. The Bible is written in unrelenting gender-exclusive language for both God and humankind. And its male bias in language appears to be consistent with its overall message regarding the relationship of the sexes. At the beginning, one finds the Adamic myth that traditionally has been translated and interpreted to legitimate male superiority. Toward the end, Paul echoes this same myth to repeat what appears to have been a consistent, androcentric tradition throughout: "A man ought not to cover his head, because he is the image of God and reflection of his [sic] glory. Woman is the reflection of man's glory. Man was not made from woman but woman from man. Neither was man created for woman but woman for man" (1 Corinthians 11:7-9). No wonder some major feminist scholars are convinced that the primary texts of Christian faith are irrevocably misogynist.

We can move beyond such first impressions, however, and the tools of critical scripture scholarship enable us to do so. We can believe that the Bible mediates the inspired word of God, but we must also recognize that it is written in very human language. As such, and like all language, it reflects the social/cultural perspectives, attitudes, assumptions, and biases of the time and place in which its oral traditions first emerged and its texts were drawn together. But modern biblical scholarship can enable us to read the text in light of its original context. In fact, by uncovering the influences of its ancient patriarchal culture, critical scholarship can enable us to discern more clearly the Bible's lasting truth for our time. *The task is to inherit and appropriate the revelatory potential of sacred scripture, while rejecting its cultural limitations and social biases as contrary to God's will and revelation.* Fulfilling this challenging hermeneutical task calls the Church, as a whole people of God, to draw upon the best scholarly resources available, and upon contemporary consciousness (through which God's Spirit also moves), and to prayerful discernment and dialogue.

Distinguishing in scripture between what is of God's word and what simply reflects its cultural context is not a new departure. We long ago rejected the Bible's three-tiered understanding of the cosmos (heaven, earth and a subterranean abyss of water) and likewise its view that the earth is the center of the universe (God be good to poor Galileo!). If we can so readily leave behind its cosmology, we can also leave behind its misogynist and sexist attitudes as a limited "world view" of the time. In fact the Bible itself has central and constitutive values of justice, shalom, love and so on, that require us not to use it to legitimate any kind of discrimination on any basis whatever.

For Humankind

The Hebrew Scriptures call a people of God to shalom and right relationship; the Christian Testament calls people to fullness of life, to radical love, and to participation in an "inclusive discipleship of equals."[1] Its androcentric language pattern and sexist tendencies notwithstanding, the overwhelming witness of the Bible is: that God created women and men in God's own image and likeness, with equal value and dignity, and intends us to be equal partners in a covenant of "right relationship" with God, each other and creation; that the praxis of the historical Jesus epitomized a heightened commitment to such mutuality and inclusion; that Jesus contravened many of the sexist mores of his culture and invited people into a radically inclusive community of disciples. Conviction and clarity about these overarching attitudes reflected in the Bible have been deepened in recent years by the work of outstanding scripture scholars with a feminist consciousness such as Phyllis Trible and Elisabeth Schüssler Fiorenza (see *Resources*). In addition, now common recognition of scholars is that the fundamental impetus of the Bible for inclusion and mutuality has been greatly diminished by its translators.

We recognize in faith that the Bible mediates the inspired word of God, but we have no cause to believe that its translators are equally inspired. In fact, the original texts are significantly more gender-inclusive than their typical translations. For example, *Strong's Exhaustive Concordance* reflects a translation of the Bible that has more than 4000 references to "man" or "men"; however, almost 3000 of them are insertions or instances where the original text clearly did not intend to be gender-specific.[2] Many central and oft-cited passages are in fact mistranslations; a notable instance is the Adamic myth.

Phyllis Trible points out that the Hebrew word *adam* as employed in the Genesis story does not have a sexual identification, and is more accurately translated generically as "earth creature" rather than "man" in the male gender sense. The terms *ish* and *ishshah*—the gender-specific terms man and woman—are not introduced until Genesis 2:23 in the second creation account, and only after the sexual differentiation of *adam,* the "earth creature." Then, the woman is presented as *ezer* which is not well translated by the traditional "helpmate" (implying subordination) but more accurately as "companion" or "partner." In fact, Trible notes, *ezer* is often used of God in relation to Israel.[3] The other frequently used term in the Hebrew Scriptures for humanity is *enosh*; like *adam,* it is not well translated as gender-specific but as "humanity" or, better still, as "mortal person."

To summarize, the Hebrew scriptures have the generic terms *adam* and *enosh* for humanity and the gender specific *ish* and *ishshah* for man and woman (*zakar* and *neqebah* also mean male and female, as in Genesis 1:27). If these distinctions were observed, as many as 200 inaccurate male referents could be eliminated from a typical translation of the Psalms alone (and thus from the prayer life of the Church), and hundreds more from throughout the Bible.

Similarly, in the New Testament *anthropos* is a nongender-specific term for person and is used constantly throughout, whereas *aner* and *gyne* are gender-specific for man and woman in general or for married people in particular. Yet translations heretofore have ignored this distinction and render *anthropos* almost invariably as "man." For example, "not on bread alone does *man* live" (Matthew 4:4), "how can a *man* be born again" (John 3:4), "a *man* is justified by faith" (Romans 3:28), should all read "person" because the original greek text has *anthropos*. Referring specifically to such words as *adam* and *anthropos*, the U.S. Catholic bishops have counseled against their traditional male translation in the lectionary texts. Walter Wink, a noted scripture scholar, states more forcefully, "The fact is that sexist translations are inaccurate. The use 'men' when women are clearly included is not just insensitive; it is incorrect."[4]

Beyond such mistranslation, one often finds instances of serious "undertranslation," especially regarding women's functions in the first Christian communities. Elisabeth Schüssler Fiorenza argues convincingly that much evidence about women's leadership has been "written out" of the Christian texts and needs to be reconstructed; but even the traces that remain are often minimized by the translation. To cite two examples from Romans 16. In verse 1, Phoebe is referred to as *diakonos*. Many versions render this not "deacon," as they do when the term is used of men, but "servant" or some other synonym. (Even "deaconess" is a derivative not called for by the text). One popular bible paraphrase refers to Phoebe as "a dear Christian woman." In Romans 16:7, Junia is called an *apostolos* but many translations, instead of "apostle," refer to her as a "missionary," a "messenger." The RSV refers to "Junias" (i.e., making it a male name) as one of "the men of note among the apostles," although *aner* is not in the text and the weight of opinion is that Junia was a woman. (The New RSV makes clear that Junia was a woman and "prominent among the apostles").

For God

The Bible has feminine (mother, midwife), masculine (father, lord), non-gender-specific (baker, potter), impersonal (rock, light), and active/agential (creator, defender) images for God. To begin with, the Bible reflects a deep awareness that all language for God is limited, and at best, analogous ("God is like a . . .," which, as analogy, implies that God is also *not* "like a . . ." at all). In fact, to make any one image the equivalent of God is to fall into idolatry. Then there is the explicit statement of Hosea 11:9 "I am God, not man (*ish*)." Beyond that, one finds throughout scripture a great variety of images, analogies, and metaphors for God (the first three verses of Psalm 18 alone has ten different ones). Undoubtedly, and to be expected in the cultural context of its time, there is a preponderance of male terms, but the fact of even one female image for God in the Bible would be significant. There are, in fact, many: *mother,* (Numbers 11:12-13, etc); *midwife,* (Genesis 1:27, etc); *woman,* (Luke 15:8-10, etc); *mother bear,* (Hosea 13:8); *mother eagle,* (Deuteronomy 32:11-12, etc); *mother hen,* (Matthew 23:27, etc), and others.

Though its gender-inclusive language for God is so significant, beyond this we should also note the even broader point of the Bible's use of what I referred to earlier as "expansive" language for God. It employs an almost endless list of images, metaphors and analogies from the life and times of its people, all seeking to name and address this One that is God., clearly aware that no one name will ever be sufficient or can ever stand as the literal equivalent. Elizabeth Johnson offers a helpful summary of the Bible's expansive language for God: some terms are "taken from personal relationships such as mother, father, husband, female beloved, companion, and friend"; others are "taken from political life such as advocate, liberator, king, warrior, and judge"; then, God is imaged from "a wide array of crafts and professions," and is portrayed as acting on the world like "a dairymaid, shepherd, farmer, laundress, construction worker, potter, fisherman, midwife, merchant, physician, bakerwoman, teacher, writer, artist, nurse, metal worker, homemaker"; and "feminist exegesis . . . brings to light the evocative vision of God as a woman giving birth, nursing her young, and dedicated to child care for the little ones"; beyond that, from the animal kingdom, God is imaged "as roaring lion, hovering mother bird, angry mother bear, and protective mother hen"; and there are images drawn "from cosmic reality such as light, cloud, rock, fire, refreshing water, and life itself."[5] Surely this Biblical witness gives us the mandate to do likewise in our time, to constantly expand our language in hopes of engaging our hearts and minds in prayer and theology that is life-giving for all, and that nurtures "right relationship" with God, among ourselves, and with God's creation.

A particular issue for Christians is the image of God as Father, clearly the favored image of Jesus (i.e., the Greek *patēr*; the much commented-on *abba* is reported in the original text as used by Jesus only once, Mark 14:36). As the liturgy states, Jesus "taught us to call God our father." In using this title, however, it is clear Jesus did not intend to teach that God is male and only male; to do so would violate the first commandment. It is equally evident that

Jesus' intent was to address God as *like* a loving, trustworthy, kind, and gentle parent. To do so, the historical context would suggest that Jesus called God "father." The assumption then was that life originates from the male parent alone. Medically, people were not aware that the mother contributes equally to conception by her ovum, and she was seen instead as solely the incubator of the male seed. Regardless of the weight of this point, it is clear that Jesus' intention in calling God "Father" was not to project patriarchy into heaven and thus to legitimate patriarchal structures on earth—surely a taking of God's name in vain. For us the crucial issue is whether or not we can still capture all that Jesus meant then by "Father" by simply repeating the term and without using other terms that help to complete what Jesus intended. (See Catechetical below).

A note on the maleness of Jesus. The historicity and particularity of Christian faith is grounded in Jesus of Nazareth, whom we confess to be consubstantial with God in divinity and with us in humanity. As for all human beings, Jesus had to be of one gender or the other, and the Gospels give no indication of any particular significance in his being male. Better, then, to treat this as one aspect of the "scandal of particularity" that was his life: as a person, Jesus was a man, a Jew, a carpenter, from Nazareth, etc. *It is through his divinity and humanity, not particularly his maleness, that Jesus is our Savior and Liberator.*

In a summary Pauline statement of the agency of Jesus in our salvation, we read: "Death came through a *person* (*anthropos,* not *aner* as typically translated); hence the resurrection of the dead comes through a *person* (*anthropos*)" (1 Corinthians 15:21). It is unfortunate and misleading when the maleness of Jesus is used to favor men and exclude women in any way. The Church appears to do so when it uses what is called "the iconic argument" against the ordination of women: that the one who represents Jesus in the moment of eucharist must have a "natural resemblance" to him. But Jesus is our representative before God because of his humanity rather than his maleness; thus any human being can be a representative of Jesus. Otherwise, Rosemary Ruether's question "Can a male savior save women?" must be answered negatively.[6] But the ancient Christian formula is that "what was not assumed (i.e., by the Christ) was not redeemed."

Clearly, Jesus in his humanity represented both men and women; conversely, both women and men can represent the Risen Christ. And that the Risen Christ is not to be limited to the maleness of the historical Jesus was a Christian conviction from the beginning; how else could Paul have used an image like "Body of Christ" to describe the Church and insist that women as well as men are invited to full membership. By baptism, both women and men are *imago Christi.*

By way of sensitivity to inclusive language, it seems advisable when referring to Jesus to emphasize his humanity rather than his maleness. A guideline from the Lutheran Church recommends: "Because characteristics associated with gender cannot sufficiently represent the true divinity or full humanity of Jesus, it is helpful to reduce reliance on gender-based pronouns."[7] In this we will be following the lead of scripture which often uses *anthropos* in preference to *aner* in referring to Jesus. For example, the centurion confessed his faith, "truly this person (*anthropos*) was the Son of God" (Mark 15:39). Even in Jesus' frequent title translated as "Son of Man," the Greek word is *anthropos.* It would seem that the *Inclusive Language Lectionary* is on good grounds in using "the Human One" as a "formal equivalent" to Son of Man.[8] A crucial confession of Christian faith from 1 Timothy 2:5 is typically translated along the lines, "One . . . is the mediator between God and men, the man Jesus Christ," but the greek has *anthropon* (people) and *anthropos.* Similarly, the Nicene Creed confession, "and became man," is not well translated since the original Greek has *anthropos*. (The Latin likewise is *homo*, not the male gender-specific *vir*). It is more faithful to the tradition and intent of the original Creed, then, for Christians to confess that this "true God from true God . . . became truly human."

Theological

The Christian Church has contributed to improving the status of women, but also has practiced and allowed its tradition to be used to legitimate sexism. It must now recognize that sexism is sinful and like all forms of discrimination is to be avoided, opposed, and eradicated.

It is important to recognize and remember that the Christian Church over its history has given witness to the dignity and equality of all people. It has struggled to remember and be faithful to what Paul declared: "There does not exist among you Jew or Greek, slave or free, male or female. All are one in Christ Jesus" (Galatians 3:28). Inspired by the egalitarian praxis of Jesus, by his call to an inclusive community of disciples, and remembering his contravening of many of the sexist mores of the time, for the first Christians the Gospel was an impetus to set aside the debased position of women in Greek and Roman culture. By comparison, over history it would seem that women have had their rights more respected and defended under the ambit of Christianity than under other "sacred canopies." Yet there is ample evidence that the Church has also and frequently failed to follow the radical witness of Jesus to inclusion and mutuality.

The first patristic authors (the "fathers" of the Church) did not withstand the misogynist influence of their surrounding culture. Some instances: Tertullian referred to women as "the devil's gateway"; Jerome raised the question whether or not women could be saved and decided, yes—by becoming men at death; John Chrysostom declared that "among all savage beasts, none is found so harmful as women"; Augustine interpreted the Adamic myth to claim that women are not in the image of God and are the source of sin through carnality, and, further, that they are to be punished by bearing children in sorrow and being submissive to their husbands. Later, Aquinas, echoing Aristotle, declared that "woman is something deficient or accidental." From the 12th to 17th centuries, witch hunts that put millions of innocent women to death had the blessing of the Church. The *Malleus Maleficarum,* an official document of the Church giving rationale and direction for the trial of witches, stated that women have a "natural tendency for witchcraft . . ."— an assumption of guilt.[9] And the instances could go on.

In our own day, the continued exclusion of women from ordained ministry in the Catholic Church is seen by fair-minded scholars as without theological or biblical warrant.[10] The challenge for the Church now is to recognize the sexism within its own life and structures, and like Peter, "the rock" it claims as foundation, to weep for its sins and make "a firm purpose of amendment." One symbolic and thus not inconsequential step in this direction would be to reform its public language patterns to be gender-inclusive of all humankind.

All God-language is analogous and metaphorical. *The first commandment forbids "graven images"* (Exodus 20:4); *to take any image of God literally is idolatrous.* The theological tradition has always been aware that all language for God is inadequate to the reality it attempts to describe. We may use analogies ("God is like . . .") but must never insist on the literal meaning of how the sentence is completed. By way of human language, as the Fourth Lateran Council taught, "God is indescribable."[11] And that Council went on to explicitly declare: "between Creator and creature, no likeness can be expressed without implying a greater unlikeness." Thomas Aquinas often echoed this sense of the inadequacy of human language and analogy for God, insisting eventually that what we claim to know of God reflects more what we can't than what we do know: "Since our mind is not proportionate to the divine substance, that which is the substance of God remains beyond our intellect and so is unknown to us."[12] Thus, far from taking our language for God literally, we must ever insist on its limitations.

Monotheism, the great central tenet of Hebrew faith, also leads to the consequent conviction that no graven image can ever be taken as the equivalent of God. This is why the First Commandment is indeed first—the mandate to let only God be God and to avoid all forms of idolatry. This foundational biblical mandate leads Elizabeth Johnson to write convincingly: "the tenacity with which the patriarchal symbol of God is upheld is nothing less than violation of the first commandment of the decalogue, the worship of an idol."[13]

Political

The exclusion or demeaning of women in language encourages similar treatment in the political realm. "If God is male, then the male is God." We already noted the power of words as symbols to propose a normative model of life, to express peoples' identity and "world" and likewise to shape the same. Here I simply highlight that this philosophical and social power of words has significant political consequences. Androcentric language works to the political and social disadvantage of women. Sharon Neufer Emswiler writes: "When a male or female is constantly bombarded with masculine terminology and masculine imagery, the result is to form the conclusion, unconsciously, that all life is lived in the masculine gender, by the male sex, thus placing the female outside the boundaries of *human* life, in a world of her own."[14]

For those who doubt the political power of gender-exclusive language, Neufer Emswiler cites a significant empirical study. She summarizes: "College students were presented with a series of statements containing "man" and "he" in a context that clearly allowed a generic interpretation of these words. Rather than responding inclusively by saying that such terms referred to either or both sexes, the students tended to identify the subjects as males. Males were selected 407 times and females only 53 times." (Note that this is a ratio of approximately 8 to 1.) She concludes: "The tendency is overwhelmingly to image male when generic language is used, even when the context would easily allow male and female."[15] Miller and Swift cite 17 different scholarly studies which indicate that "man," "men," and the pronouns "he," "him," and "his" are heard or read by the great majority of people as gender-specific and "tend to call up images of male people only, not female people or females and males together."[16]

For religious language too, we must recognize that there are serious political consequences, and debilitating ones for women, in constantly referring to God in exclusively male imagery. Such powerful public symbolism promotes maleness as normative on every level of existence—personal, interpersonal, and social/political. Elizabeth Johnson summarizes well: "Patriarchal God symbolism functions to legitimate and reinforce patriarchal social structures in family, society, and church."[17] Or, in the oft-quoted and pithy phrase of Mary Daly: "If God is male, then the male is God."[18]

Liturgical

Our worship is the true measure of what we believe and teach. Liturgical symbols are the most formative of all because of their "aura of ultimacy." Of all language, the language of worship should encourage us in "right relationship" with God and each other. There is a time-honored formula in the Church of "lex orandi, lex credendi." Translated literally it means "the law of praying, [is] the law of believing." It reflects the conviction that the liturgy is the norm and measure of Christian faith. To appreciate this point I refer again to what was said in

Chapter 1 about symbols. Liturgy is above all a symbolic event, and the language world it creates is constitutive of its symbolic power. But the old theological dictum that "the sacraments effect what they symbolize" is apparently more than a confession of faith. Clifford Geertz, writing as an anthropologist, claims that of all symbols, liturgical ones are potentially the most formative and transformative of people's self-identity because they have "an aura of ultimacy" to them; they propose and help to "effect" an "ultimate model" of reality.[19] Conversely, we can presume, liturgical symbols that are inadequate to the life-giving intent of liturgy, are likely to malform people and distort communities; they encourage a distorted sense of self, world, and God.

Vatican II referred to liturgy, and to the eucharistic liturgy in particular, as "the summit toward which the activity of the Church is directed; at the same time it is the fountain from which all [its] power flows"; and, "the Eucharistic Action is the very heartbeat of the congregation of the faithful."[20] How crucial it is, then, that the Church celebrate a liturgy that is inclusive and sacramentally adequate to the lives of all its participants, that its "public work" portray to people life-giving images of themselves, of God, and of how to live as a people of God.

Even a moment's reflection helps us to realize that of all language surely the language of shared prayer and liturgy ought to nurture "right relationship" with God and each other. It is precisely this concern for people's spirituality that demands precisely this concern for people's spirituality that demands exceeding care in the language of worship. Here Jane Redmont is insightful: "What has brought many women, and some men, to protest the privileged use of male God-language is not the desire to be politically correct, but the desire for God." Care for the "lex orandi" reflects "at least three concerns: the desire that our common praise not lead us into idolatry, but toward justice; the care that the way we name God and ourselves not injure our companions; and the hope that these words, and the holy silence beneath them, will lead us to God."[21]

It seems imperative for the very sacramentality of the liturgy, that the language world it creates for people be gender-inclusive.

Catechetical

Catechists can help end sexism in Church and society by not teaching it, and by teaching for inclusion and mutuality. Much of what has already been said, as well as much of what follows in Chapter 3, pertains to the language pattern of catechists and religious educators.

Here I emphasize the obvious point that one way to help put an end to sexism in Church and society is to stop passing it on, to stop teaching it. We can presume, of course, that very few catechists intend to pass on sexist attitudes and disvalues to their students through their "explicit" curriculum. But we can teach it by our "null" curriculum (what we choose *not to teach*) and by our "implicit" curriculum (what we *inadvertently teach*). Our language pattern is *the* most eminent instance of our implicit curriculum, what we teach "incidentally" by the way we talk about people and God, and about how to live as a people of God. It is so crucial, then, that the Church's catechetical language, for so many people their first source of formal religious language, be gender-inclusive.

In this regard, one must note with great regret that the first officially approved English translation of the *Catechism of the Catholic Church* does not reflect commitment to inclusive language. This is a needless distraction from the real intent and, I believe, the rich potential of the *Catechism* for the catechetical ministry of the Church. It seems all the more offensive in that the first proposed translation was at least sensitive to this issue but then was "corrected" to reflect male dominance and patriarchy in its language pattern. However, I believe that we could make either of two inappropriate responses to this translation: one would be to accept its insensitivity without protest; the other would be to dismiss or sideline the *Catechism* because of its exclusive language. And we can be confident that this translation will not be the final one. Bernard Cardinal Law of Boston, who has championed the efforts for a gender sensitive translation, has been quoted as saying "that there will be a later Latin edition . . . When that appears, I am certain that there will be revisions in all future language translations." Meanwhile, as we work for a "better day," we can highlight the unequivocal teaching of the *Catechism* itself that "God created and willed man and woman in perfect equality as human persons . . . Man and woman are both in the image of God with equal dignity" (#369). Likewise, we can take heart from its declaration that beyond the traditional image of Father, "God's parental tenderness can also be expressed by the image of motherhood . . . It is fitting to recall that God transcends the human distinction between the sexes. God is neither male nor female, just God, who transcends human fatherhood and motherhood" (#239).

An issue of particular concern for catechists is the strong tradition in primary catechesis of referring to God exclusively as "Father." (This is often occasioned by the teaching of the Creed, the Lord's Prayer, the Sign of the Cross, and the "Glory Be"). As already noted, if "Father" is the only image used of God, and especially in early catechesis, it may no longer teach what Jesus intended to teach with this analogy. For too many children in our society, fathers are absent, emotionally unavailable, or even abusive. On catechetical grounds alone, one must question the advisability of posing God *exclusively* as "Father." Note well: I don't believe the problem is with calling God "Father" but will calling God *only* "Father"—the sole metaphor for God. In all catchesis, early or late, we have the challenge of offering expansive language for God!

One possible solution (which for this author has seemed successful with younger children) is to interchange the terms "father," "mother," and "loving parent" for God. Then, when teaching a traditional prayer like the "Our Father," teachers can take care to explain in the catechesis which follows that Jesus intends us to approach God as a trustworthy, forgiving and loving *parent.*

I also note the caution that some authors make to be sparing and careful in using all parental images for God. For example, Hardesty writes: "the images of God as mother and father can be deeply meaningful. On the other hand, all of us also know the adolescent's need for independence, for a separate individual identity. We must also be very careful not to project our distorted, sexist family patterns onto God, patterns of oppression of husbands over wives, parents over children."[22] For me this caution simply highlights again the need for expansive language, that catechetically we cannot rely unduly on any one image or even genre of images for God.

There are, I'm sure, many other "reasons" for shifting to inclusive language beyond the eight categories outlined above. However, the most compelling reason for Christians must surely be the "great commandment" of love. With charity as "the supreme law," strategies for how to proceed will occupy us in Chapter 3.

Questions for Conversation

Take note of something you particularly agreed with, disagreed with, or might add to the above reflections.

Note and give the reasons for your response to the statement, "If God is male, then the male is God."

What do you envision as some practical steps toward inclusive language in catechesis and liturgy?

— 3 —

Implementing
Gender-Inclusive Language

Questions for Conversation

Reviewing the rationale offered in the previous two chapters, and using a scale of 1 to 10
(1 = totally opposed, 10 = totally in favor), indicate your own position on the issue of gender-
inclusive language. Explain why you now take
the position you choose.

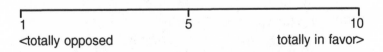

1   5   10
<totally opposed   totally in favor>

When you imagine the "next generation" of
Catholic Christians, what are your hopes for
them regarding inclusive language? How can
you help in the realization of your hopes?

"Charity is the Supreme Law"

At the heart of Christian faith is the conviction that "God is love" (1 John 4:8), and that "the greatest commandment" is the "law of love" (See Matthew 22:38-40, etc.). More recently we have renewed our conviction and heightened our consciousness that the love preached by Jesus was deeply rooted in his Hebrew tradition of faith that does justice. When Jesus spoke of love, he meant love that both demands and is built upon justice as "right relationship"—with God, self, others and creation; justice especially for the poor, oppressed, marginalized, and those to whom life is most denied. Exclusive language can encourage "wrong relationship" and does not reflect love that does justice. On this often polemical issue, it is wise to recall "love that does justice" as our "supreme law" in order: a) to suggest *the* ultimate rationale for change, and b) to establish the spirit that should guide us in the transition to inclusive language.

That such love is the most compelling reason for change was epitomized for me in a remark by a then octogenarian priest-friend (since gone home to God) who was most conscientious about using inclusive language when he presided at liturgy. When I inquired what had convinced him to alter so significantly the language he used for both God and persons, he confessed that he did not quite understand *why* so many people now find exclusive language offensive but decided to change because of a comment of his grand-niece. She had told him that her awareness of sexist language had made the mass an alienating experience, and that it was becoming increasingly difficult for her to attend. "That," he said, "convinced me to change. I would never want anyone to feel alienated by the words I use when I preside at mass." Here was "the law of love" at work!

This "supreme law" should be reflected in our approach as a Christian community as we push on toward language patterns that are horizontally gender-inclusive (when speaking of persons) and vertically both gender-inclusive and expansive (when using analogous personal language for God). Love, of course, sometimes demands resistance and "hard sayings." But for "right relationship" love also calls for perseverence while posing alternatives, for understanding of how peoples' traditions have shaped their attitudes while refusing to acquiesce in those traditions, for self-reflection instead of self-righteousness, for strategic prudence that encourages even gradual improvements instead of insisting on instant "puritanism," and so on. But even as loving and right relationship with God, neighbor, and self is the ultimate reason why we make this effort to change, and likewise is the spirit of how to proceed, we are still in need of concerted strategies to adjust both our own and our community's language patterns.

The following suggestions are far from exhaustive, some do not have any consensus as yet, and the proposals I make may only suggest other or better possibilities. I categorize my recommendations by focusing, a) on language about persons, b) on "God-talk," and c) on the particular and perhaps "hardest case" of liturgical language.

Regarding Ourselves

Here I propose three guidelines: *1) Avoid linguistic omission of women when the intention is to include them; 2) Use positive and respectful rather than negative and demeaning identifications for women; 3) Avoid stereotyping the sexes and limiting the roles in which women and men can function.* Clearly these guidelines often overlap.

1) Avoid omission

This pertains especially to the allegedly generic but in fact androcentric terms for humankind. For instance: when both genders are intended, use humanity, humankind, women and men, people, etc., instead of man, men, mankind, etc.; likewise, use he/she or s/he instead of he; use one's, her/his or his/hers instead of his.

When possible, favor the plural to allow the gender-inclusive pronouns—their, them, they. For example, instead of "the doctor . . . he" or "the nurse . . . she" (which are also stereo-types), use "doctors or nurses . . . they."

Important to note here is that the U.S. National Council of Teachers of English have de-creed that it is now permissible to use they, them or their to refer an indefinite singular pronoun (a return to the practice of middle English). Thus, contrary to how we were taught, instead of saying "everyone knows he is to decide for himself," it is now considered acceptable grammar to say "everyone knows they are to decide for themselves." Or, as Shakespeare would and did say it, "God send everyone their heart's desire."

To avoid omission, use terms like "manufac-tured" instead of "man-made," "first year" in-stead of "freshman," "workforce" instead of "manpower," "human achievements" instead of "man's achievements," "ancestors" instead of "forefathers," "community" instead of "fellow-ship," and so on. Avoid the man/men ending unless only man/men are referred to; for "sales-men" use "salespeople," for policemen use po-lice, and so on. Use "parenting" instead of "mothering" when the former is intended. (It is interesting to note that "to mother" has meant to nurture, whereas "to father" has meant only the very limited and transitory act of insemination).

Avoid using "man" as a verb, as in "to man a project"; instead, use "staff," "work at," etc. Avoid using "man" as an adjective; instead of "be man enough to tell the truth," say "have the courage to tell the truth."

For words that have "man" as a middle syllable, use synonyms: instead of "sportsmanlike" use "fair play," for "workmanlike" use "skillful," and so on. Be careful, too, of Latin words that are traditionally used with masculine gender when both male and female are intended: e.g., instead of alumni use "alumni/ae," or better, perhaps, "alums."

2) Avoid demeaning

One common form of "put-down" language is to define a woman in relation to some man. There are many ways to change this. Some instances and possibilities: "man and wife" can be "spouses," "wife and husband" (or vice versa); Mrs. John Smith can be Mary Smith (unless she uses her pre-marriage name), Mrs. O'Neill and John Smith should be Mary O'Neill and John Smith; housewife can be homemaker, and so on.

It can also imply the inferiority of women to consistently name them after men; for example, vary the "traditional" order from men and women, boys and girls, husbands and wives, to women and men, girls and boys, wives and husbands.[1]

Avoid trivializing terms like "pretty co-ed" (use, instead, "bright student"), "spinster" (use "single woman"), "career girl" (use "professional woman"). And avoid demeaning phrases like "the good woman behind the successful man," "I will have my girl type it." In fact, avoid "girl" when referring to any adult woman.

It seems generally agreed that all the "-ess" words (waitress, actress, etc.) are demeaning as derivatives because they imply a male standard and a female modification. Avoid them. The same pertains to the suffixes "-ette" (e.g., usherette; use usher) and "-trix" (e.g., executrix; use executor).

Other instances that imply a male norm are likewise to be avoided (overlaps again with stereotyping): e.g., avoid woman doctor, lady lawyer, woman theologian, and so on.

"Working woman" can demean the work of women within the home; use, e.g., "salaried woman." Avoid phrases like "old wives' tale" (use, e.g., superstition), and nick-names like "tom-boy" for a girl or woman (considered a compliment) or "sissy" for a boy or man (usually an insult). And there are countless other instances of demeaning language.

3) Avoid stereotyping

So much of our language about people in the professions and services reflects sexual stereotyping in that it limits roles to either men or women, typically favoring men as the norm. In addition to avoiding the qualifiers as noted (e.g., woman theologian), use terms like firefighter, postal worker, sailor, supervisor, and ordained minister, instead of fireman, mailman, seaman, foreman, clergyman, and so on.

There is also an opinion that for such traditionally "man" ending terms it is best to specifically name the sex of the person referred to, that simply replacing "man" with "person" still leaves women invisible. For example, when referring to a particular person, use chairwoman/man, congressman/woman, spokeswoman/man, according to the person's gender; thus, chairperson, etc., is preferred only when the referent is indefinite.

Avoid professional stereotyping too, as in "the doctors and their wives . . . .," "the teachers and their husbands," etc. A basic rule in avoiding such stereotyping is not to limit the kinds of work that women or men can do.

Another common form of stereotyping limits the affective characteristics of both women and men: avoid "women are . . . emotional, soft, tender, follow their hearts, etc," and likewise "men are . . . hard-headed, tough, insensitive, etc."

Avoid the trivializing and put-down stereotypes: e.g., women as back-seat drivers, naggers, spend-thrifts, etc.; likewise, men as sports nuts, uncultured, can't cook, etc.

There is also a pattern that makes very different evaluative judgments of behavior which is common to both men and women. For example, resourceful men are often referred to as "ambitious and independent" (considered appropriate), whereas similar women are called "aggressive and pushy" (a put-down). Think through and avoid such demeaning stereotypes!

Give parallel treatment to the sexes; e.g., avoid identifying women by marital status, number of children, etc., unless men are similarly noted.

A basic principle that should be followed, except in cases of biological function (e.g., giving birth), is that all statements made, stories told, etc., should be capable of having the sex roles reversed, i.e., women and men should be designated as capable of doing the same things.

There are also some peculiar personifications along gender lines that are better avoided: e.g. "mother nature," "father time," "the Church . . . she" (use "it").

Regarding God

In Christian faith, God is not the impersonal force of deism but the personal God revealed in God's relationship with the people of Israel and in the person Jesus, the Christ. While we may have illuminating (but always inadequate) formulations to speak theologically of God, (e.g., Tillich's "Ground of Being"), everyday religious speech and especially prayer require personal language for God. How else can we speak with faith *about* or *to* the One we believe to be in triune relationship with us and within God-self? (In traditional theological language, the economic and immanent Trinity.) And yet, so much of our personal language is gender-specific. The challenge is to use personal God-language that analogously reflects all humanity and the "indescribable" (Fourth Lateran Council, 1215) mystery of God.

It seems well advised to follow the biblical pattern of expansive language: *use gender-inclusive (parent, friend), gender-varied (interchange father and mother or use mother/father), non-gender-specific (potter, shepherd), agential (defender, creator), or, on occasion, nonpersonal (rock, fortress) images, metaphors and analogies for God.*

Likewise, we should avoid male pronouns for God—his, him, he, himself—and instead repeat the word God again in a sentence, or use "the divine," Godself, God's very self, God's own, etc. From personal experience of public speaking and writing, I'm convinced that male pronouns for God can be avoided without undue circumlocutions and while honoring the aesthetic of the language.[2]

Similarly, some biblical titles or referents for God can be readily made gender-inclusive: Sovereign One can be used instead of Lord, or Sovereign God instead of Lord God; reign or realm of God can be used instead of kingdom; God as ruler can be used instead of king.

Regarding the Trinity, I have already proposed that Jesus' humanity rather than maleness be emphasized. Further, I believe that male identification and referents for the Risen Christ can and should be avoided since our faith is that the Risen One represents all humanity. Concerning the Holy Spirit, the term for spirit in Hebrew and Aramaic, Jesus' native tongue, is *ruach* (also means breath or wind) and is feminine in gender, and the Greek word is *pneuma* and neuter. Thus the original texts advise that we not use male imagery or pronouns for the Holy Spirit.

Regarding how we name the Persons of the Blessed Trinity together, *we face a particular challenge to honor the intent of the Trinitarian formulas of apostolic faith handed on and confessed by the Church*—and yet *to be gender-inclusive.* Some responsible scholars are convinced that the terms "Father, Son and Holy Spirit" are essential to express the Church's Trinitarian doctrine concerning the interrelationship within the Godhead. For example, Daniel Helminiak argues for the traditional terms on the ground that: "Titles that do not imply a relation of origin do not preserve the distinction of subjects in God. 'Creator' sets up no relations between those in God; rather it implies a relation between God and creatures."[3] However, why the "relations" within the Godhead must be conveyed only by male terms is not clear to me! Furthermore, diversity and adjustment of Trinitarian language is not new in the history of the Church.

In our own time we have experienced a precedent of altering the Trinitarian formula from Holy Ghost to Holy Spirit. And within the tradition there are countless instances of inclusive language for God and the Trinity. For example, William of St. Thierry (c.1085-1148) wrote of God as mother. Julian of Norwich (c.1342-c.1413), a very influential English mystic, wrote of the Trinity as "the Creator, and the lover, and the protector" of all creation, as "almighty, all wise, and all good," and as "sovereign power, sovereign wisdom, and sovereign goodness."[4] She frequently referred to God and to Jesus as "Mother," and said of the Second Person, "the deep wisdom of the Trinity is our Mother, in whom we are enclosed."[5] A central image of Julian for human existence was to say that we dwell in the womb of God—a deeply feminine image of the divine.

The liturgy, echoing 2 Corinthians 13:13, refers to "the grace of Jesus Christ, the love of God and the (communion) of the Holy Spirit." Beyond this, we need imagination to find a gender-inclusive and readily usable expression of the Trinity that is theologically faithful to the ancient formulas of Christian faith. *Terms like "Creator, Savior and Sanctifier" seem worthy candidates, at least when speaking of the Trinity's relationship to us* (i.e., the "economic" Trinity). A formula that might more adequately represent our faith in the triune relationship within the Godhead (i.e., the "immanent" Trinity) is suggested by an inclusive-language breviary text which prays *"Glory to you, Source of all Being, Eternal Word, and Holy Spirit . . . ."* And there will be many other proposals to be tested by time and the "sense of the faithful."

Regarding Liturgy

The "guidelines" already recommended are eminently relevant to the liturgical language of a Christian community. However, the language world that the Church creates in this central "public work" deserves special consideration, and with some urgency. For everyone, it is the most formative language of their faith, and for most it is our regular encounter with religious language.

The Latin "typical edition" of the *Roman Missal,* published in 1969 in response to Vatican II, has gone through at least four significant revisions. The Sacramentary section of the missal has had two different major translations and is now in the process of a third (which promises to be "gender-sensitive"). This makes the point that the liturgical language of a Christian community is and should be constantly revised in order to adequately symbolize its faith in the midst of changing times, and to do so with beauty and resonance to people's lives. While it is true that the Catholic communion does not possess an officially approved, gender-inclusive Sacramentary and Lectionary at this time (and may be as much as five years away), there is historical precedent for making the needed changes. We can also take heart that the International Commission on English in the Liturgy (ICEL), the agency which represents as many as 14 bishops' conferences and supervises the translation of all official liturgical texts from Latin to English, made a commitment as early as 1975 to inclusive language in the liturgy. While their subsequent proposals are still ahead of their episcopal constituencies, and even further ahead of approval by the Vatican's Congregation for Divine Worship, some progress has been made at "official" levels.[6]

In 1975, the U.S. National Conference of Catholic Bishops (NCCB) officially approved use of "for us and for all" in the words of consecration over the wine (replacing "for all men," the previous translation of *pro multis*). In 1981, the Congregation for Sacraments and Divine Worship "ratified" the same. Given the traditional Catholic appreciation for the words of eucharistic institution, this was a significant intimation of concern for inclusive language in worship; people who appreciate the power of symbols should not underrate it. Some more recent Latin texts have been translated with inclusive language (e.g., Rite of Commissioning of Special Ministers of Holy Communion, 1978). Now, as throughout the history of the Church, by building upon what is possible today the *vox populi* can help nudge Church officialdom to new ways of acting tomorrow. Comments on each of the central linguistic components of the mass—1) readings, 2) order and propers, and 3) hymns—will indicate some instances of opportunity. (The guidelines already recommended pertain especially to the language for preaching).

1) Readings

It is important to first note that any lectionary is a *selection* of readings from the Bible; it includes some passages from scripture but leaves out many others. Clearly the Church's principle of selectivity should be to choose a set of readings that best reflects and nurtures its people's faith. Vatican II said as much regarding the Roman Lectionary: "The treasures of the Bible are to be opened up more lavishly, so that richer fare may be provided for the faithful at the table of God's Word. In this way a more representative portion of the holy Scriptures will be read to the people over a set cycle of years."[7] Likewise, the Introduction of the present Roman Lectionary states that its intent is to "present the more important biblical passages . . . the more significant parts of God's revealed Word." However, there is evidence that the present Lectionary, last revised in 1981, is seriously flawed by its minimizing of women's roles in salvation history.

Martha Ann Kirk, who has done significant research on the representation of women in the

Roman Lectionary, summarizes: "The persons working on . . . selecting the 'more important biblical passages' have generally left out stories of women." She continues: "Less than 10 percent of the Sunday and feastday readings deal with stories of women; and the stories that are used are almost all ones of women being helped, healed, or rescued, or stories that focus on the biological role of women as bearers of male children." Even when women's stories are included, they are often assigned to weekdays and are thus heard by fewer people. Kirk notes, "Scripture describes powerful, influential women, such as Deborah, Judith, Esther, and Ruth. Not one of these is ever used in the Catholic lectionary on Sundays or major feastdays."[8]

In some of the stories of women chosen for the Lectionary, it would seem that representation of their courage and faith is deliberately deleted. For example, in Chapter 1 of Exodus, the Pharaoh tells the midwives Shiphrah and Puah, "When you act as midwives for the Hebrew women and see them giving birth, if it is a boy, kill him; but if it is a girl, she may live" (v. 16). The women disobey the pharaoh's edict because they know it is against God's will (v. 17). When challenged, they give Pharaoh a lame excuse: "The Hebrew women are not like the Egyptian women. They are robust and give birth before the midwife arrives" (v. 19). Regretfully, this instance of women's faith and courage is not included in the Lectionary. The story is partially included beginning with Exodus 1:8, but verses 15-21— precisely the section describing women's faith and courage—are deleted and the reading continues with verse 22.[9] It is to be hoped that the revision of the Roman Missal now underway will correct such "absence" and "deletion" of women from the Lectionary selections.

Working with the present Lectionary, in the vast majority of Catholic parishes the readings (and thus the missalettes, if used) are based on the New American Bible (NAB) translation. One good reason is that of all the translations, the NAB seems the most suitable for public reading and proclamation; a less worthy reason is that the copyright is owned by the NCCB. Unfortunately, the NAB is extreme in its exclusive language, not only "vertically" but also "horizontally," with many originally inclusive words translated exclusively, and androcentric terms added to the text. This prompts many communities and readers who are committed to gender-inclusive language into the ad hoc arrangement of rephrasing the readings as printed. While this exigency is created by the circumstances and at times can be done quite readily (e.g., changing "men" to "people") it is clearly not a "solution." To do it well, while being faithful to the intent of the original text, is an awesome task that not even the best trained biblical scholars would attempt "on their feet."

In this "ad hoc" situation, the U.S. Catholic Bishops have issued some guidelines for the language of the scripture readings at Mass. In a document entitled "Inclusive Language in Liturgy: Scriptural Texts," they establish two guiding principles, first: "Biblical translations must always be faithful to the original language and internal truth of the inspired text" (#9); and, on the other hand, "every effort should be made to render the language of biblical translations as inclusively as a faithful translation of the text permits." (#14)[10]

Meanwhile, as we await approval by Rome of a "gender sensitive" lectionary submitted by the U.S. Catholic Bishops, Catholic parishes should be aware that they have other choices. To begin with, the New Jerusalem Bible (1985) is a translation officially approved for use in Catholic worship. In this re-presentation of the Jerusalem Bible, the translators have significantly reduced the so-called "generic" male language. Likewise, there is now available and approved by the National Conference of Catholic Bishops a recasting of the New Testament of the New American Bible. Its attempt at inclusive language is minimalist; however, in the Preface it states: "When the meaning of the Greek is inclusive of both sexes, the translation seeks to reproduce such inclusivity insofar as this is possible in normal English usage. . . ."[11] One must be grateful for all signs of progress!

Beyond this, *there are also available at least three widely used lectionaries that reflect inclusive language to different degrees.* Two are based on the Revised Standard Version (RSV), a translation officially approved for Catholic lectionary; the third, from the Quixote Center, reflects the New American Bible and so has more appeal in Catholic parishes. The most inclusive and adventuresome is *An Inclusive Language Lectionary* (See *Resources*), produced by a committee of eminent scripture, theological and pastoral scholars under a mandate from the National Council of Churches. Used widely now in mainline Protestant congregations that follow the Common Lectionary, the ILL is gender-inclusive both horizontally and vertically, while giving readers an "option" on the latter. In references to God, it places additions to the original text in parentheses, as in "God the Father (and Mother)." When it departs from the RSV on a key term, as for example by favoring Sovereign, it places the former term in parentheses, as in "(or Lord)." Its attempts at vertical inclusion, however, have brought the ILL a fair share of controversy; some scholars challenge, for example, its use of "The Human One" instead of "Son of Man" as a title for Jesus.

Also available is the *Lectionary for the Christian People,* which follows the common lectionary of Catholics, Episcopalians and Lutherans. It portrays itself in the Introduction as less radical than the ILL, and "conservative in its maintenance of key biblical imagery."[12] However, it is inclusive toward humankind, it avoids all male pronouns for the divine, and it reduces the instances of male imagery for God. Lastly, Priests for Equality, based at the Quixote Center in Washington, has now published all three cycles of an inclusive-language lectionary.[13]

2) Order, Propers

The Order is made up of the features that are a consistent aspect of every mass (the Holy, Holy, Lamb of God, etc.), and the Propers are the prayers—collects—that are particular to each day. The present Order seems to sin boldly against inclusive language, even horizontally. That God is male who made man and saves men is constantly repeated, in one way or another.[14] The variable prayers of the Propers (opening, over gifts, after communion) are usually horizontally inclusive in that they are spoken in the first person plural (we ask . . . help us, etc); however, with very few exceptions, their English translation addresses God as Father or Lord. Again, this preponderance of male imagery for God is at least in part the responsibility of translators. In the original Latin text, *Pater* is used only 21 times (in over 1400 prayers); yet the English version inserts "Father" in 560 collects. (The argument made is that "God" as direct address presents euphony problems; but why not "Loving God," etc?) Likewise, "Lord" is frequently added beyond the Latin text.[15]

Within the present Roman Missal there are also "instances of possibility." A rubric in the present Order at the "Pray Brethren . . ." (toward end of Offertory) notes: "At the discretion of the priest, other words which seem more suitable under the circumstances, such as friends, dearly beloved, brothers and sisters, may be used." In other places, the rubrics note that the celebrant "may use these or similar words." The General Instruction at the beginning of the Sacramentary has a distinct tone of flexibility, often rating things to be used "as appropriate." It seems, then, that the Sacramentary itself does not encourage a rigorist approach to its prayer wordings, greetings, etc. More importantly still, surely the "supreme law" of love must prevail over any linguistic rubric, if fulfilling the latter would exclude or alienate people at the moment when all should feel most included and in "right relationship" as the Body of Christ.

The present "typical edition" of the Roman Missal was composed before consciousness about inclusive language; further we anticipate a new and more inclusive translation within the next five years. In this time of transition, then, I'm convinced that: *All presiders and ministers at mass or communion services can address and lead the assembly in prayers that are gender-inclusive for both God and ourselves. Likewise, people can pray their common prayers and responses inclusively.* No presider need address God only as "Father" in the collects, or say of Jesus in the Fourth Eucharistic Prayer "a man like us . . . ." Why not "person"? Here again, presiders who so choose need not rely solely on their own creativity. In 1980, ICEL prepared the nine eucharistic prayers in inclusive language. This publication (*Eucharistic Prayers*, see Resources) was approved by the bishops' conferences of the U.S. and Canada, and submitted to Rome for "confirmation," (which it still awaits). Henderson writes, "The present position (regarding this publication) of the Congregation for Divine Worship is that the inclusive language emendations proposed . . . will be considered in the context of the larger project of the revision of the Missal."[16]

Engaging people to pray and participate at liturgy with inclusive language will clearly take some educational efforts and perhaps printed suggestions for the congregation. For example, the presider can readily say, "Pray sisters and brothers, that my sacrifice and yours will be acceptable to God our loving parent." The people can respond: "May God accept the sacrifice at your hands for the praise and glory of God's name, for our good, and the good of all the Church." (The German Sacramentary offers such an alternative along-side the "official" form). Given how deeply etched the traditional formulas are in many people's minds, it is important not to force uniformity but to welcome for now a bit of "varieties of tongues" (1 Corinthians 12:10) in communal praise of God.

Again, however, rather than each congregation presuming to adapt the language of the Order according to its own lights, there is now available for consideration a version of its principal prayers that are horizontally inclusive and avoid male pronouns for God. This is from the English Language Lectionary Committee, and is published as *Praying Together* (See *Resources*). The ELLC is a broad-based ecumenical group on which the Catholic Church is represented by its International Commission on English in the Liturgy (ICEL).

A further sign of hope on the horizon for Catholics is that ICEL is now preparing a new translation of the "typical edition" of the Roman Missal (previous translation 1975). It promises to be consistently gender-inclusive on a horizontal level, and vertically to eliminate male pronouns and to decrease the male imagery for God.

3) Songs

The 25 years since Vatican II have seen an extraordinary increase in congregational singing by Catholic parishes during liturgy. It was probably Luther who first perceived the "educational" power of hymns that every congregant can sing. Because singing engages us emotionally and aesthetically, the faith and theology that we express in song is powerfully formative of our Christian identity. What people sing they are likely to "learn by heart" and long remember. We can add to the old adage, "to sing is to pray twice—and to be much influenced by what we sing." *Our songs at liturgy should be gender-inclusive to reflect the mutuality of all humankind and the mystery of God.*

In the aftermath of Vatican II there was an explosion of creativity among Catholic composers that has continued unabated. Most of them are now sensitive to inclusive language. However, the first of the new Church music was composed before this consciousness was widespread, and so, regretfully, some of the earlier compositions are gender-exclusive. The question is what to do about them, since many have become favorites. (Some composers are rewording earlier work, e.g., Brian Wrenn, see *Resources* below). A strict interpretation of copyright law dictates that they be sung as copyrighted. But there seems to be an unwritten agreement on the part of composers and publishers to allow congregations to change at least the more egregious language in this regard.

Happily, an increasing number of inclusive-language hymnals are becoming available (see *Resources*) They include some that have attempted to recast "old favorites" accordingly (see especially, *Everflowing Streams*). For example: "Praise God from whom all blessings flow; Praise Christ the Word in flesh born low; Praise Holy Spirit evermore; One God, Triune, whom we adore."[17]

Amen.

Questions for Conversation

Out of all these reflections and your dialogue with "neighbors," how do you articulate your own strongest convictions now regarding gender-inclusive language?

Are there some commitments that you feel called to make at this time?

Are there actions you would like to take with others in your community of faith? How can you proceed together?

Endnotes

Preface

1. See my *Sharing Faith,* esp. Ch. 4, for a more thorough description of a "shared Christian praxis" approach (San Francisco: Harper and Row, 1991). Hereafter cited works that are general resources will receive only a brief note; full publishing data can be found under Resources at the end.

Chapter 1

1. Miller and Swift, *The Handbook of Nonsexist Writing,* p. 4.

2. Hardesty, *Inclusive Language in the Church,* p. III.

3. The mandate of the National Council of Churches to the Inclusive Language Lectionary Committee was to seek "language which expresses inclusiveness with regard to human beings and which attempts to expand the range of images beyond the masculine to assist the church in understanding the full nature of God." *An Inclusive Language Lectionary* (hereafter *ILL*), Year A, p. 10.

4. See *Guidelines* from United Methodist Church in Resources below.

5. Miller and Swift, *Nonsexist Writing,* p. ix.

6. Hardesty, *Inclusive,* p. 15.

7. Spender, on whose research I rely here, makes the point that the correlation in language between alleged male superiority and male social power is more than circumstantial; its historical roots are evident especially in the structure of the language. See *Man-Made Language,* pp. 138-151, for this and the historical notes that follow.

8. See Miller and Swift, *Nonsexist Writing,* p. 45.

9. Spender, *Man-Made Language,* p. 2.

10. Ibid, p. 139-140.

11. Miller and Swift, *Nonsexist Writing,* p. 4.

Chapter 2

1. This oft-cited phrase is from the work of Elisabeth Schüssler Fiorenza. She argues convincingly that it was the original intent of Jesus. See, *In Memory of Her,* p. 154 and passim.

2. See Hardesty, *Inclusive Language in the Church,* pp. 79-82.

3. See Trible, *God and The Rhetoric of Sexuality,* p. 91, for this point, and p. 75ff for her commentary on the second creation account.

4. Walter Wink, "The New RSV: The Best Translation, Halfway There," *The Christian Century,* 107:26, Sept. 19-26, 1990, p. 830. In their statement entitled "Inclusive Language in Liturgy: Scriptural Texts," the U.S. Catholic bishops offer the following guideline to avoid such mistranslations: "Words such as *adam, anthropos* and *homo* have often been translated in many English biblical and liturgical texts by the collective terms man

and family of man. Since in the original languages these words actually denote human beings rather than only males, English terms which are not gender specific, such as person, people, human family and humans should be used in translating these words." (#19)

5. Elizabeth Johnson, *She Who Is,* p. 118. See also Virginia Ramey Mollenkott, *The Divine Feminine*, for an excellent review of the biblical imagery of God as female.

6. Ruether, *Sexism and God-Talk*, Ch. 5.

7. Evangelical Lutheran Church, *Guidelines,* p. 16.

8. See *Inclusive Language Lectionary*, Year A, p. 251-252.

9. See Ruether, *Religion and Sexism,* for the references for these and many more historical instances of sexism in the Jewish and Christian traditions.

10. Official Catholic statements usually offer three arguments against the ordination of women: 1) that there were no women among "the twelve"; 2) that it would be contrary to the tradition; 3) that to represent Jesus, a priest must be male (the "iconic argument"). For a fine, balanced and scholarly refutation of these arguments, see, for example, Rahner, *Concern for the Church,* Chapter 3.

11. See *The Church Teaches: Documents of the Church in English Translation,* (Rockford, IL: Tan Books, 1973), p. 132.

12. Thomas Aquinas, *De Potentia,* (Westminster, MD: Newman Press, 1952), q.7, a.5.

13. Elizabeth Johnson, *She Who Is,* p. 39.

14. Neufer Emswiler, *Women and Worship,* p. 5.

15. Ibid., p. 13-14.

16. Miller and Swift, *Handbook of Nonsexist Writing,* p. 13; see pp. 168-170, for bibliography on these studies.

17. Johnson, *She Who Is*, p. 36.

18. Mary Daly, *Beyond God the Father,* p. 19.

19. Clifford Geertz, "Religion as a Cultural System," in *Anthropological Approaches to the Study of Religion,* Michael Banton, ed., London: Tavistock Pub., 1966.

20. *Documents of Vatican II*, Abbott, ed. p. 142 and 542.

21. Jane Redmond, "Pronouns, Poets, and the Desire for God," *America,* March 16, 1991, pp. 298 and 299.

22. Hardesty, *Inclusive,* p. 31. See also Plaskow, *Sin, Sex and Grace,* pp. 162-167.

Chapter 3

1. On the issue of "ordering," Miller and Swift write: "Some linguists theorize that it is easier to say a single-syllable word like *men* than a two-syllable word like *women*, and that we tend to put the single syllable first as a result. Another theory is that the order has something to do with prosodic patterns: since 'men and women' and 'male and female' scan as two trochees, they trip more lightly off the tongue than they would if reversed to scan as a trochee and an iamb. Neither theory accounts for *husbands and wives* or such other familiar phrases as *coffee and cake, needle and thread, hammer and tongs, fathers and sons,* or—to get to the root of the matter—*Adam and Eve*." *Handbook of Nonsexist Writing,* p. 117.

2. In authoring three catechetical series, grades K. to 8 (i.e. 27 student texts), I found it readily possible to avoid male pronouns for God without detriment to the aesthetic of the prose. See *The God With Us, Coming to Faith* and the Revised *Coming to Faith* programs from W.H. Sadlier.

3. Daniel Helminiak, "Doing Right by Women and the Trinity Too," p. 119. See also Louis Roy, "Inclusive Lan-

guage Regarding God"; Donald G. Bloesch, *The Battle for the Trinity,* pp. 39-41.

4. Julian of Norwich, *Showings*, pp. 131, 132, 164.

5. Ibid., pp. 279, 298, 294, 285.

6. See the excellent review essay by J. Frank Henderson, "ICEL and Inclusive Language."

7. "Constitution on the Liturgy," Abbott, ed., *Documents of Vatican II*, p. 155.

8. Martha Ann Kirk, *The Prophetess Led Them In Praise,* pp. 79, 82, and 89.

9. Ibid., p. 83. I am indebted to Kirk's research for this whole section on the androcentrism of the Lectionary selections.

10. See "Inclusive Language in Liturgy: Scriptural Texts" #23 for an interesting application of these two principles to adjusting pronouns.

11. Preface to the Revised Edition, *The New American Bible,* St. Joseph Edition, New York: Catholic Book Publishing Co., 1988, p. 6.

12. *Lectionary for the Christian People,* p. xi.

13. This lectionary is available from Priests For Equality, Box 5243, Hyattsville, MD 20782.

14. Kirk writes: "The texts for people and priest for Eucharist for an average Sunday have from fifty to sixty male metaphors for God the Creator and no female metaphors." *The Prophetess,* p. 76.

15. See Henderson, "ICEL, etc.," p. 274.

16. Ibid., p. 273. (Parenthesis added)

17. *The Book of Worship,* United Church of Christ, p. 66.

Resources

Philosophical and Theological

Bynum, Carol W. *Jesus As Mother: Studies in the Spirituality of the High Middle Ages.* Berkeley: Univ. of California, 1982.

Cameron, Deborah. *Feminism and Linguistic Theory.* New York: St. Martin's Press, 1985.

Carr, Anne E. *Transforming Grace: Christian Tradition and Women's Experience.* San Francisco: Harper and Row, 1988.

Coll, Regina, ed. *Women and Religion: A Reader for the Clergy.* New York: Paulist Press, 1982.

Daly, Mary. *Beyond God the Father: Toward a Philosophy of Womens Liberation.* Boston: Beacon Press, 1973.

Fiorenza, Elisabeth Schüssler. *In Memory of Her: A Feminist Theological Reconstruction of Christian Origins.* New York: Crossroads, 1983.

_____. *Bread Not Stone: The Challenge of Feminist Biblical Interpretation.* Boston: Beacon Press, 1984.

Hardesty, Nancy. *Inclusive Language in the Church*. Atlanta: John Knox Press, 1987.

"Inclusive Language: Do We Need It?" *Daughters of Sarah*, Jan-Feb 1985, entire issue.

Johnson, Elizabeth. *She Who Is: The Mystery of God in Feminist Theological Discourse*. New York: Crossroad, 1993.

Julian of Norwich. *Showings*. New York: Paulist Press, 1978.

Kirk, Martha Ann. *The Prophetess Led Them In Praise: Women's Stories in Ritual*. Doctoral Dissertation: Graduate Theological Union, Berkeley, May, 1986.

McCloskey, Pat. *Naming Your God: The Search for Mature Images*. Notre Dame, IN: Ave Maria, 1991.

McFague, Sallie. *Models of God*. Philadelphia: Fortress, 1987.

_____. *Metaphorical Theology: Models of God in Religious Language*. Philadelphia: Fortress, 1982.

Mollenkott, Virginia Ramey. *The Divine Feminine: The Biblical Images of God as Female*. New York: Crossroads, 1984.

Plaskow, Judith. *Sex, Sin and Grace*. Washington, D.C.: Univ. of America Press, 1980.

Ruether, Rosemary Radford. *Sexism and God-Talk: Toward a Feminist Theology*. Boston: Beacon Press, 1983.

_____. *Religion and Sexism: Images of Women in the Jewish and Christian Traditions*. New York: Simon and Schuster, 1974.

Russell, Letty. *Feminist Interpretation of the Bible*. Philadelphia: Westminster, 1985.

_____. ed. *The Liberating Word: A Guide to Non-Sexist Interpretation of the Bible*. Philadelphia: Westminster, 1976.

Sawicki, Marianne. *Faith and Sexism: Guidelines for Religious Educators.* New York: Crossroads, 1979.

Spender, Dale. *Man-Made Language.* Boston: Routledge & Kegan Paul, 1980.

Swidler, Leonard. "Jesus Was A Feminist," in *New Catholic World,* Jan., 1971. (A dated but still groundbreaking essay).

Trible, Phyllis. *God and the Rhetoric of Sexuality.* Philadelphia: Fortress, 1978.

_____. *Texts of Terror: Literary-Feminist Readings of Biblical Narratives.* Philadelphia: Fortress, 1984.

Wahlberg, Rachel Conrad. *Jesus According to a Woman.* New York: Paulist Press, 1975.

Guidelines

Canadian Conference of Catholic Bishops. *Inclusive Language.* Ottawa, Ont.: CCCB, 1990.

Guidelines for Inclusive Use of the English Language for Speakers, Writers and Editors. (1989) Evangelical Lutheran Church of America: 8765 W. Higgins Rd, Chicago, IL 60631.

Guidelines for Eliminating Racism, Ageism, Handicappism and Sexism. (1983) United Methodist Church General Council, Dayton, OH.

Guidelines for Equal Treatment of the Sexes. (n.d.) New York: McGraw-Hill Book Co.

Maggio, Rosalie. *The Non-Sexist Word Finder: A Dictionary of Gender-Free Usage.* New York: Oryx Press, 1989.

Miller, Casey and Kate Swift. *The Handbook of Nonsexist Writing.* San Francisco: Harper and Row, 1988 (2nd ed.).

National Conference of Catholic Bishops, *Inclusive Language Translations: Scriptural Texts for Liturgy.* Washington, D.C.: USCC, 1990.

Resources for Liturgy

Clark, Linda, Marian Ronan and Eleanor Walker. *Image-Building: A Handbook for Creative Worship with Women of Christian Tradition.* New York: Pilgrim Press, 1981.

Duck, Ruth C. and Michael Bausch. *Everflowing Streams: Songs for Worship.* New York: Pilgrim Press, 1981.

Duck, Ruth C. *Flames of the Spirit: Resources for Worship.* New York: Pilgrim Press, 1985.

Eucharistic Prayers, (1980), a provisional text; limited copies available from ICEL, 1275 K St., N.W., Suite 1202, Washington, D.C. 20005.

"Excellent Words: Inclusive Language in Liturgy and Scripture" Prepared by Lutheran and Episcopal Campus Ministries, M.I.T.: Cambridge, MA 1988.

Faull, Vivienne and Jane Sinclair. *Count Us In—Inclusive Language in Liturgy.* Nottingham: Grove Books, 1986.

Guide to Inclusive Hymn/Song Resources. Annotated bibliography developed by UMC; send self-addressed, stamped envelope to GCSRW, 1200 Davis St., Evanston, IL 60201.

Henderson, J. Frank. "ICEL and Inclusive Language" in *Shaping English Liturgy: Essays in Honor of Archbishop Denis Hurley.* Peter Finn and James Schellman, eds. Washington, D.C.: Pastoral Press, (1990).

Hearing the Word: An Inclusive-Language Liturgical Lectionary. Washington, D.C.: St. Stephen and the Incarnation Episcopal Churches. 1982.

Huber, Jane Parker. *Joy in Singing.* Atlanta: Presbyterian Church (USA), 1983.

An Inclusive-Language Lectionary, Years A, B & C. Prepared under sponsorship of National Council of Churches of Christ, USA. Published by John Knox, Westminster, & Pilgrim Presses. 1983-86.

"The Inclusive Language Lectionary, Cycles A, B, and C." Available from Priests for Equality, Box 5243. Hyattsville MD 20782.

Lectionary for the Christian People, Years A, B & C. Gordon Lathrop and Gail Ramshaw. Published by Pueblo Pub. Co. and Fortress Press, 1986-87.

Liberating Liturgies from Women's Ordination Conference, P.O. Box 2693, Fairfax, VA, 22031-1989.

Neufer Emswiler, Sharon and Thomas. *Women and Worship: A Guide to Nonsexist Hymns, Prayers and Liturgies.* San Francisco: Harper and Row, 1984.

Praying Together. English Language Liturgical Consultation. Nashville: Abingdon Press, 1989.

Proctor-Smith, Marjorie. *In Her Own Rite.* Nashville: Abingdon Press, 1993.

Ramshaw, Gail. *Worship: Searching for Language.* Washington, D.C.: Pastoral Press, 1988.

Ruether, Rosemary Radford. *Women-Church: Theology and Practice of Feminist Liturgical Communities.* San Francisco: Harper and Row, 1986.

Schreck, Nancy and Maureen Leach. *Psalms Anew: A Non Sexist Edition.* From Sisters of St. Francis, Dubuque, IA, 1984.

Sleevi, Mary Lou. *Women of the Word.* Notre Dame, IN: Ave Maria, 1989.

Watkins, Keith. *Faithful and Fair: Transcending Sexist Language in Worship.* Nashville: Abingdon, 1981.

Wrenn, Brian. *Faith Looking Forward: The Hymns and Songs of Brian Wrenn.* Carol Stream, IL: Hope Press, 1983.

Wrenn, Brian. *What Language Shall I Borrow?* New York: Crossroad, 1990.

Voices of Reserve

Many fine essays and monographs have been published that oppose or have serious reservations about the move toward inclusive language. I have been challenged by the following:

Bloesch, Donald G. *The Battle for the Trinity: The Debate Over Inclusive God-Language.* Ann Arbor, MI: Servant Publications, 1985.

Helminiak, Daniel. "Doing Right by Women and the Trinity Too," *America,* Feb. 11, 1989.

MacMaster, Eve. "Is 'Inclusive Language' Theologically Sound, Or Just This Year's Fashion?" *America,* Feb. 2, 1991.

Roy, Louis. "Inclusive Language Regarding God," *Worship,* 65:3, May 1991.